THE BALTIMORE RAVEN

A Championship Poem

Copyright ©2023 Robert Bowie Johnson, Jr.

Solving Light Books
727 Mount Alban Drive
Annapolis, MD 21409

ISBN: 9798863617305

SolvingLight.com

For Nancy Lee

Special Thanks to
Beth Johnson Fisher

Last play of the 1958 Colts-Giants NFL Championship overtime game in New York. Halfback Lenny Moore throws a key block as fullback Alan Ameche, after getting a handoff from quarterback Johnny Unitas, scores the winning touchdown, giving the Colts a hard-fought 23 to 17 victory.

INTRODUCTION

THE COLTS AND THE RAVENS

Most knowledgeable pro football fans consider the Colts-Giants championship battle in 1958, the first overtime game in NFL history, the "greatest game ever played." Nationally televised by NBC and witnessed by 40 million viewers, the game sparked the popularity of professional football during the 1960s. The Baltimore Colts thrilling victory set the standard for great football.

In March of 1984, frustrated by inconclusive stadium negotiations, Colts owner Robert Irsay, under cover of darkness, abruptly moved the team to Indianapolis.

In 1996, after twelve seasons without an NFL team, the Ravens franchise arrived in Baltimore. Four years later, head coach Brian Billick led the Ravens to a Super Bowl victory in 2001 defeating the New York Giants, 34-7. And in 2013, head coach John Harbaugh led the Ravens to a second Super Bowl victory defeating the San Francisco 49ers 34-31. That great Baltimore Colt championship spirit is back home where it belongs.

EDGAR ALLAN POE'S *THE RAVEN* BECOMES *THE BALTIMORE RAVEN*

In 10th grade English class at Baltimore Poly, when it was still on North Avenue, we studied the works of Poe. I loved the power and brilliance of *The Raven.* So did Poe himself. Even before publication in 1845, Poe knew he had a sensation on his hands. When a friend described an early reading of the poem as "fine, uncommonly fine," Poe immediately responded: "Is that all you can say for this poem? I tell you it's the greatest poem ever written."

I agree with Poe. I memorized all eighteen verses, quoting it often at parties to the delight of the hearers.

When the Ravens came to town, I overwrote Poe's masterful poem as a tale of championship triumph, thankful that "Baltimore" and so many other key words rhyme with nevermore.

Even now, when I read *The Baltimore Raven* aloud, this part of verse XIII, reminiscent of Chuck Thompson's play-by-play announcing, still chokes me up. How could anyone who ever heard it not remember:

. . . Chuck's smooth voice so rich and
Deep, so proud and sure:
"Unitas drops back, he looks deep,
                There's Lenny Moore!"

The boundless exhilaration of those electrifying, breathtaking moments! That great Baltimore Colts spirit now animates the Baltimore Ravens, so "Let's go you Baltimore Ravens and put the ball across the line."

                              RBJ, Jr.
                              October 2023

CHARACTERS IN
THE BALTIMORE RAVEN POEM

VERSE V

Eugene Allen "Big Daddy" Lipscomb, 6' 6" tall and weighing 284 pounds, played alongside Hall of Famers Gino Marchetti and Art Donovan, and was instrumental in the Colts' two consecutive NFL championships in 1958 and 1959.

VERSE VI

Gino Marchetti, defensive end for the Colts from 1953 to 1966, fought in the Battle of the Bulge as a machine gunner during World War II. Sid Gilman, the Los Angeles Rams head coach called Gino "the greatest player in football," adding that "It's a waste of time to run around this guy's end. It's a lost play. You don't bother to try it." The Pro Football Hall of Fame inducted Gino in 1972.

Art Donovan, inducted into the Pro Football Hall of Fame in 1968, excelled as a defensive tackle for the Colts. Artie served as a Marine during World War II, taking part in the fierce battles of Luzon and Iwo Jima. Artie made a key tackle during the overtime of the 1958 championship game, stopping the Giants and allowing Johnny Unitas to lead the Colts on an 80-yard scoring drive to win the game.

Verse VII

Johnny Unitas, one of the greatest NFL quarterbacks of all time, led the Colts to four championship titles. Between 1956 and 1960, he set the record for most consecutive games with a touchdown pass at 47, standing for 52 years. A three-time NFL most valuable player with ten Pro Bowl and five first team All-Pro honors, the NFL inducted Johnny U into their Hall of Fame 1979.

Verse XI
The "unhappy master," Baltimore Colts team owner Robert Irsay who snuck the Colts out of town to Indianapolis during a snow storm in March of 1984.

Verse XIII
Chuck Thompson, According to Colts and Orioles fans America's all-time greatest sportscaster and play-by-play announcer. Chuck loved to exclaim—and we loved to hear it—"Ain't the beer cold!"

Lenny Moore, Halfback and flanker Lenny Moore thrilled the fans from 1956 to 1967. Selected to the Pro Bowl seven times, the Pro Football Hall of Fame inducted him in 1975.

Verse XVII

Bill Pellington, a beloved and feared linebacker who played a key role in the 1958 and 1959 NFL championship victories.

Mike Curtis, Four-time Pro Bowler who excelled in sacks and interceptions in his ten years with the Colts, 1965 - 1975.

Raymond Berry, One of the greatest receivers of all time, inducted into the Pro Football Hall of Fame in 1973. The passes he caught from Johnny Unitas in the Colts' final 80-yard drive in their overtime victory over the Giants for the 1958 NFL championship are legendary.

Jimmy Orr, Popular wide receiver. Fans referred to the corner of the end zone in Memorial Stadium where he caught many of his passes as Orrsville.

THE BALTIMORE RAVEN

A Championship Poem

By Robert Bowie Johnson, Jr.

I

Once upon a midnight dreary, while I
Pondered weak and weary,
Over the departure of the Colts
From Baltimore,
While I nodded, nearly napping,
Suddenly there came a tapping,
As of someone gently rapping,
Rapping at my clubroom door.
"Some football fool," I muttered,
"Tapping at my clubroom door—
    Only this and nothing more."

II

Ah, distinctly I remember, it was
Crunch time in December;
And no team could raise my spirits
As the Colts had done before.
Eagerly I wished the morrow—
Vainly I had sought to borrow
From memorabilia surcease of
Sorrow for the lost Colts of Baltimore,
For the proud and valiant team that
Thrilled me with each score—
        Absent here for evermore.

III

And the thought of cheering on the
Redskins chilled me—filled me with
Emotions never felt before;
So that now, to still the beating of my
Heart, I stood repeating
"Is it a Colt Corralster tapping sadly
At my clubroom door—
Another baffled fan—angry, sorry,
And pigskin poor?"
Or could this be what we've been
                          Praying for?

IV

Presently my soul grew stronger,
Hesitating then no longer,
"Sir," said I, "or Madam, truly your
Forgiveness I implore,
But the fact is I was napping, and so
Gently you came rapping,
And so faintly you came tapping,
Tapping at my clubroom door,
That I scarce was sure I heard you"—
Here I opened wide the door—
    Darkness there and nothing more.

V

Deep into that darkness peering, long
I stood there wondering, dreaming—
Oh, those times Big Daddy just
Wouldn't let the other team score!
But the silence was unbroken, and
The stillness gave no token,
And the only words there spoken:
"The Colts are gone from Baltimore."
This I whispered, and an echo murmured
Back, "The Colts are gone from
Baltimore."
    Merely this and nothing more.

VI

Back into my clubroom turning, with
Memories of Gino and Artie a-churning,
Soon again I heard a tapping somewhat
Louder than before.
"Surely," said I, "surely that is
Something in my window well;
Let me see, then, what thereat is, and
This mystery explore—
　　　'Tis the wind and nothing more!"

VII

Open here I flung the shutter, when,
With many a flirt and flutter,
In there stepped a stately Raven of
The saintly days of yore.
Not the least obeisance made he;
Not a moment
Stopped nor stayed he;
But perched upon my bust of Johnny,
Just above my clubroom door—
Perched and sat,
                And nothing more.

VIII

Then this ebony bird beguiling my sad
Fancy into smiling,
By the powerful and stern determination
Of the countenance it wore,
"Though thy crest be sleek and shaven,
Thou," I said, "are sure not craven,
You wise and agile ancient Raven
Feasting on this Chesapeake shore—
Reveal thy message, make it quick, my
Heart is sore."
Then the bird said,
    "The Ravens win in Baltimore."

IX

Much I marveled this majestic fowl to
Hear discourse so plainly,
Though its answer little meaning,
Little relevancy bore;
For we cannot help agreeing that no
Living human being
Ever yet was blessed with seeing bird
Above his clubroom door—
Bird or beast upon Johnny's sculpted
Bust above his clubroom door, saying
      "The Ravens win in Baltimore."

X

But the Raven, sitting nobly on
Johnny's bust spoke only
Those five words, as if his soul in
Those five words he did outpour.
Nothing farther then he uttered—not a
Feather then he fluttered—
Till I scarcely more than muttered,
"Other teams have flown before—
On the morrow you will leave me, as
Our team left town before."
    Quoth the Raven: "Nevermore."

XI

Startled at the stillness broken by
Reply so aptly spoken,
"Doubtless," said I, "what it utters is
Its only stock and store,
Brought from some unhappy master
For whom stadium disaster
Followed fast and followed faster till
His mal-intent one abrupt action bore:
Take the Colts from Baltimore."

XII

But the Raven now beguiling my
Curiosity into smiling,
Straight I pushed my recliner in front
Of bird, and bust, and door;
Then, upon the leather sinking, I
Betook myself to linking
Fancy unto fancy, thinking what this
Triumphant bird of yore—
What this trim, poised, unbridled bird
Of yore—meant in croaking
      "The Ravens win in Baltimore."

XIII

Thus I sat engaged in guessing, but
No syllable expressing
To the Raven whose fiery eyes now
Burned into my bosom's core;
This and more I sat divining, with my
Heart a-thump and pining
For Chuck's smooth voice so rich and
Deep, so proud and sure:
"Unitas drops back, he looks deep,
                There's Lenny Moore!"

XIV

Then, methought, the air grew denser,
Perfumed by a magic censer,
Swung by gridiron angels whose
Foot-falls tinkled on my red tiled floor.
"Trickster," I cried, "why do you tease me
About the lost Colts from Baltimore?
Tell me, oh, tell me, how shall we ever
Those glory days restore?"
Then the bird said,
      "The Ravens win in Baltimore."

XV

"Prophet!" said I, "thing of wonder!
Prophet still, if bird or phantom!
Whether tempter sent, or whether
Tempest tossed thee here ashore,
Insistent and sure undaunted,
In this town by Irsay haunted,
Tell me truly, I implore, is football
Back on the Chesapeake shore?"
Quoth the Raven,
    "The Ravens win in Baltimore."

XVI

"Prophet!" said I, "bird of fortune—
Prophet still of mirth and more!
By that heaven that bends above us—
By that God we both adore—
Tell this fan with expectation growing,
If, what you speak you're knowing,
Our Sundays loud again with the
Championship roar,
Alive with great defense and the last
Second score."
Then the bird said,
    "The Ravens win in Baltimore."

XVII

"Be those words the sign of blessing,
Bird of greatness, the future
Confessing—linebackers as tough as
Pellington and Curtis, receivers as
Shrewd as Berry and Orr!
I take a black plume as a token of that
Truth thy soul hath spoken!
Leave my happiness unbroken!
Adorn the bust above my door!
Lay thy beak across my heart—let's
Hear it again:
         'Touchdown Baltimore!'"

XVIII

And the Raven, never flitting, still is
Sitting, still is sitting
On that treasured bust of Johnny just
Above my clubroom door,
And his eyes are the picture of a
Victor—contenders creaming,
And the lamp-light o'er him
Streaming casts his image on the floor,
And my joy from out that image
Leaps for what's in store:
 The Ravens win it all for Baltimore!

Author's Web Sites:

Genesisingreekart.com

Ancient Greek religious vase and temple art does not depict myth. It boasts of the triumph of the way of Cain in the post-Flood world.

Powerphrases.net

A study of ideas and a stimulant to deep and original thinking.

Broadneckhundred.com

Illustrated history of the Broadneck Peninsula, 1649 to 1977.

Broadneckbaloney.com

One of the funniest books you'll ever read.

Marylandandtheconfederacy.com

What really happened based on original documents and sources.

Atruergod.com

The Supreme Spirit of Light and Love as revealed in the Hebrew and Greek Scriptures.

———